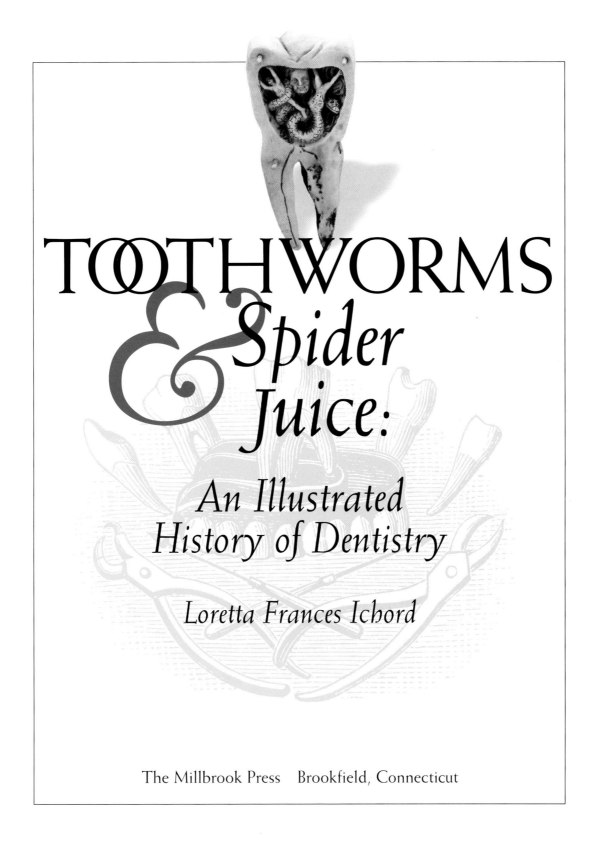

TOOTHWORMS
&Spider Juice:

An Illustrated History of Dentistry

Loretta Frances Ichord

The Millbrook Press   Brookfield, Connecticut

For my husband, William, and my three sons,
James, Andrew, and Joshua, whose smiles warm my heart.

Acknowledgments

I would like to thank Joyce A. Prange, the assistant director of Development and Public Affairs at The Dr. Samuel D. Harris National Museum of Dentistry, for her pleasant and informative tour of the museum. Also a big thank-you to The Dr. Samuel D. Harris National Museum of Dentistry for providing valuable resources in the form of graphics and historical information.

A special thanks and appreciation go to my employer for the past fourteen years, Dr. Robert R. Cushing, D.D.S., and all the wonderful dental team I work with—Cidália, Gail B., Gail M., Gail S., Jennifer, Judy, Julie, Laura F., Laura M., Lonna, Mary, and Natalie—for their unfailing support of and joy in my literary successes.

Cover photograph courtesy of Bundeszahnärztekammer
Photographs courtesy of The Granger Collection, New York: pp. 11, 15; Masters and Fellows of Trinity College, Cambridge: p. 18; Art Resource, NY: pp. 25 (Foto Marburg), 33 (Giraudon), 40 (left: Erich Lessing); Musee de l'Homme: p. 26; Bibliothèque national de France: p. 35; Without Effort, 1781 (color engraving) by French School (18th century), Private Collection/Bridgeman Art Library, London/New York: p. 37; Universitäts-Bibliothek Basel: p. 40 (right); Musée de l'Ecole Dentaire de Paris: p. 44; Photo Researchers/SPL: p. 46; Culver Pictures: pp. 49, 82; The University Museum of Pennsylvania, Philadelphia: p. 53; The New York Academy of Medicine Library: p. 63; National Library of Medicine: p. 67; Temple University Dental Museum: p. 72; The Francis A. Countway Library of Medicine, Boston, Massachusetts: p. 75; Ritter Dental Manufacturing Company: p. 78; Museo Nacional de Antropologia: p. 85

Library of Congress Cataloging-in-Publication Data

Ichord, Loretta Frances.
Toothworms and spider juice: an illustrated history of dentistry/
by Loretta Frances Ichord.
p. cm.
Includes bibliographical references and index.
Summary: Surveys the history of dentistry, from ancient
civilizations up to the knowledge and treatments of modern times.
ISBN 0-7613-1465-2 (lib.bdg.)
1. Dentistry—History—Juvenile literature.
[1. Dentistry—History.] I. Title.
RK30.I24 1999
617.6'009—dc21 99-13758 CIP

Published by The Millbrook Press, Inc.
2 Old New Milford Road
Brookfield, Connecticut 06804

Visit us at our Web site: http://www.millbrookpress.com

CONTENTS

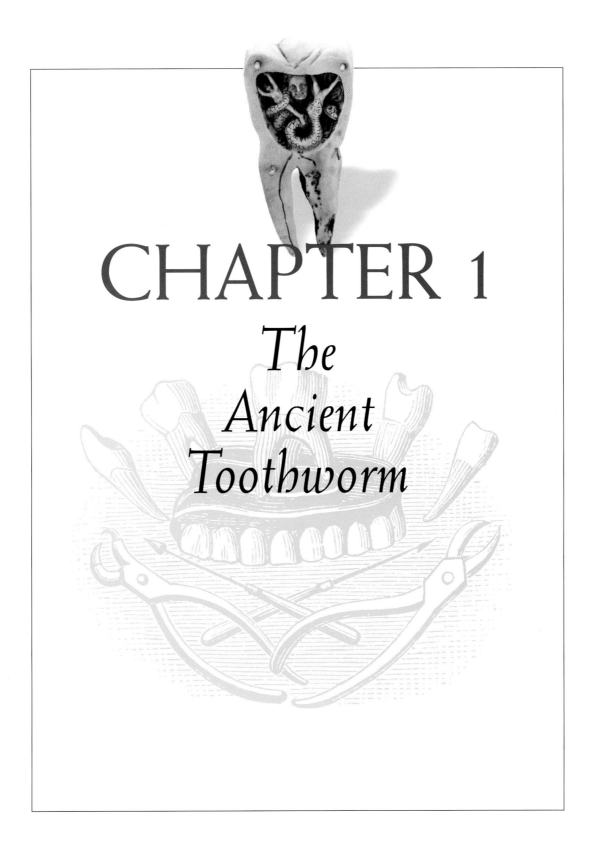

CHAPTER 1
The
Ancient
Toothworm

If you have ever suffered from a throbbing tooth-ache or been around someone who has, then you know how painful an infected tooth can be. Your only thought is to find the nearest dentist and get some relief. In ancient times and throughout the Middle Ages, people experienced many toothaches—but they had no dentists, as we know them today, to help them.

How do we know that people who lived long ago had dental problems? Teeth outlast all other skeletal remains because they have an outer layer of enamel, which is the hardest substance in the human body. Historians and scientists have found partial skulls and jaws full of teeth, some more than 5,000 years old, in burial grounds, tombs, and other sites of early civilizations. Information gathered from the study of these teeth has shown historians that people of ancient times did indeed have missing, crooked, or impacted teeth, and many suffered from decay in the teeth they had left. The ancient remains even indicate what sort of dentistry, if any, was done.

Another good source of dental information came from paintings on the inner walls of tombs and writings on clay tablets, and later on papyrus. It was from all these records that we discovered the ancient belief in the toothworm.

People of these earlier times believed that the stabbing pain of a toothache was caused by a toothworm, which either had appeared spontaneously or had bored its way into the tooth. If the tooth pain was severe, it meant that the worm was thrashing about, but if the aching stopped, then the worm was resting. Cultures all

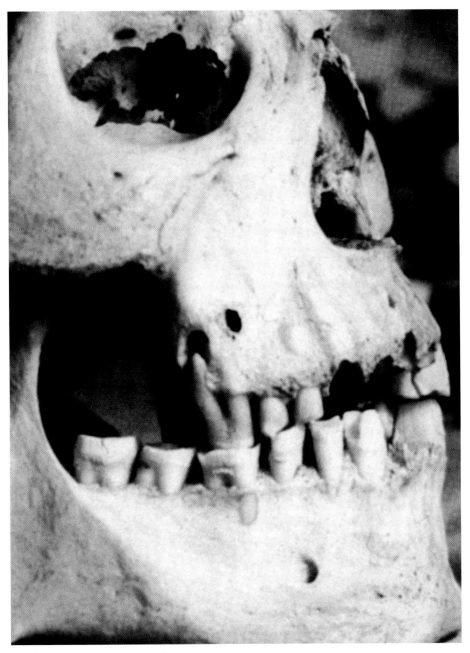

The upper surfaces of the teeth of this ancient Egyptian skull, found at Deir el Bahari, are worn away. Scientists theorize that the attrition resulted from eating bread containing abrasives from the crude millstones used to grind the flour.

over the world, many of whom had no contact with each other, held stubbornly to this myth. The folklore of the toothworm persisted from ancient times to the beginning of the eighteenth century.

The first recounting of the toothworm was found in the royal library in Babylonia. Inscribed in cuneiform on a Sumerian clay tablet (about 3000 B.C.) was a bleak poem:

> After Anu (had created heaven)...
> The earth had created the rivers,
> The rivers had created the canals,
> The canals had created the marsh,
> The marsh had created the worm.
> The worm went weeping, before Shamash,
> His tears flowing before Ea:
> "What wilt thou give me for my food?
> What wilt thou give me for my sucking?"
> "I shall give thee the ripe fig and the apricot."
> "Of what use are they to me, the ripe fig and
>   the apricot?
> Lift me up and among the teeth
> And the gums cause me to dwell!
> The blood of the tooth will I suck,
> And of the gum will I gnaw the roots!"

Had these ancient people actually seen a toothworm? Modern historians think that early civilizations may have thought the pulp inside a tooth was a worm. It is a moist, limp tissue with a wormlike appearance.

The toothworm folklore was easily believed in early societies because of their strong faith in magical and religious elements. Demons were thought to inhabit the body. No one knew that bacteria caused infection in the body and teeth. In the thinking of the time, if people had a toothache, then they probably deserved it because they had displeased the demons.

Bizarre and gross remedies were used to sicken and drive out the evil spirit that had turned itself into a dirty worm inside the tooth. One remedy involved holding in the mouth a juicy concoction made of spiders, eggshells, and oil boiled together until reduced to one-third of its volume. Another method involved building a wall around a decayed tooth with wax and then filling it with an acid solution. Today we know that if any relief was experienced after using these harsh mixtures, it was because the nerves in the pulp had died.

In ancient Egypt, tooth disease afflicted many, including the Pharaohs. One reason was their coarse diet. The grain used for bread, a mainstay of the Egyptian diet whether people were rich or poor, was ground on rough stones with many small particles of grit mixed in with the flour. In addition, the vegetables they ate were grown in a sandy soil, which added more roughness to their meals. This coarse Egyptian food made teeth wear down on the biting surfaces, exposing the pulp and resulting in abscesses and toothaches.

Another reason the ancient Egyptians had so much trouble with their teeth was that they didn't clean them often enough. Many Egyptian skulls were found to have suffered major bone loss resulting from the heavy calculus (tartar) on their teeth. No attempts appeared to have been made to remove these hard deposits.

Other ancient cultures, such as the Hebrews (about 1000 B.C.), highly valued sound, healthy teeth. The mouth was considered the doorway to the body and was to be kept scrupulously clean to protect whatever entered from contamination.

The Hebrews advised against using too much vinegar, which they believed was harmful to the teeth. But if the gums were infected, then vinegar and wine were used to heal them. The Hebrews, however, still had many toothaches. They recorded, in the Talmud, a whole list of remedies, including old wives' tales and gross cures, for painful teeth.

In ancient Greece (about 287 B.C.), as in other world cultures, the practice of oral hygiene was slow in coming. It was considered a virtue for men to shave frequently and have white teeth, but regular dental care was not known in Greece until it became a Roman province in 146 B.C. Under Roman influence, the Greeks learned how to clean their teeth. Greek physicians began to recommend that every morning people should rub their gums and teeth with their fingers and use ground mint, inside and out, to remove food particles.

In ancient Rome, Celsus (about 25 B.C.–A.D. 50) was a famous encyclopedist who compiled information about many subjects. In his text *On Medicine*, considered the most outstanding medical work of Rome, Celsus offered valuable medical and dental information, including tips such as rinsing the mouth with fresh water in the morning. But many of the Romans still suffered from periodontal disease and toothaches. Celsus left behind a handwritten book describing bleeding gums, loose

A copper engraving of Celsus, the Roman encyclopedist whose book on medicine contains descriptions of a tonsillectomy, heart attacks, and insanity, as well as many descriptions and proposed cures for dental diseases.

teeth, gums separated from teeth, and ulcers around the teeth. For bleeding gums, he recommended chewing on unripe pears and apples, making the fruit juices go into the infected gums and then washing the juices away with weak vinegar and astringents like alum. If that didn't work, then his next treatment was to cauterize (sear) the ulcerated gum with a red-hot iron.

Another celebrated Roman, the great naturalist Pliny the Elder (A.D. 23–79), wrote prescriptions that sound silly to us now. Pliny said: "To stop toothache bite on a piece of wood from a tree struck by lightning," and "Touch the tooth with the frontal bone of a lizard taken during a full moon." Other advice given by Pliny was to find a frog in the light of the full moon, pry its mouth open, spit into it, and say, "Frog, go, and take my toothache with thee!" Pliny did not guarantee that these treatments would work.

Because communication was limited in ancient times and the printing press had not been invented, most of the medical and dental advice prescribed by Pliny, Celsus, and others influenced only the people around them.

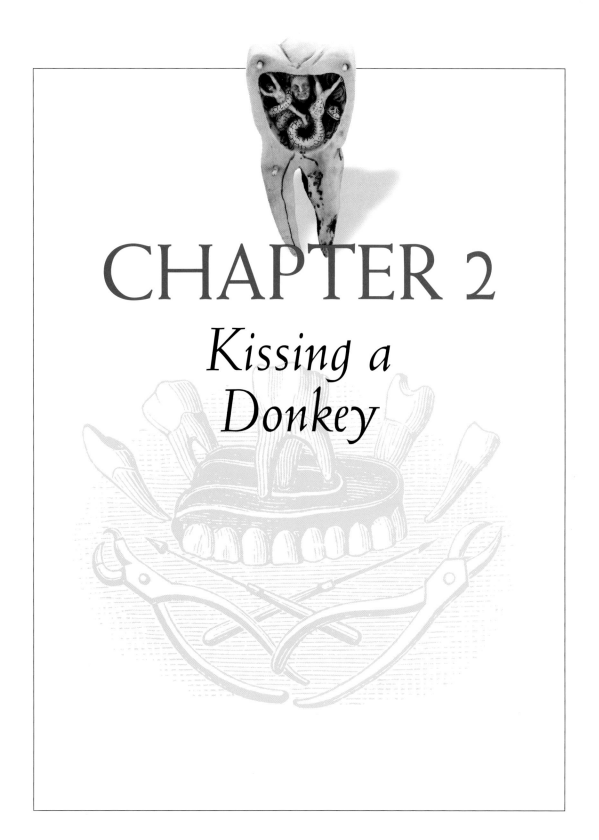

CHAPTER 2

Kissing a Donkey

For thousands of years, dental knowledge was so primitive that most people depended on folk prescriptions from their families and neighbors whenever they had a toothache.

Centuries ago, a person could sit by a well-traveled road with a handkerchief tied around his face (a universal sign of suffering from a toothache) and get advice from every passerby on how to get rid of the dreaded toothworm. There would be as many different recipes and prescriptions as there were advisers.

In this chapter a few of these historical treatments for toothaches are divided into five basic groups: Animals and Insects; Plants and Roots; Human Organs and Secretions; Inorganic; and The Transference of Toothache. Many of these prescriptions and recipes sound so strange—they appear to be poking fun at superstitions or magic. But these remedies, no matter how odd or cruel, were taken seriously. Early civilizations were open to any suggestions that might relieve them of tooth pain, considered to be the worst of tortures.

ANIMALS AND INSECTS

Bee: Honey, a product of bees, was used to coat an infected tooth in the Middle Ages. People smeared their aching teeth with honey and waited all night with tweezers in hand, ready to pluck out the toothworm. Honey used alone or in combination with other ingredients was considered one of the oldest folk medicines against toothaches. It is mentioned as a dental treatment in an Egyptian medical scroll known as the Ebers Papyrus.

This is a wood engraving from the nineteenth century, but the practice of tying a handkerchief around the jaw had been around for centuries. The medical purpose is unclear, but it does successfully draw attention to the fact that the person is suffering from a toothache.

Donkey: In ancient Greece, donkey's milk was used as a mouthwash to strengthen the gums and teeth. In the Middle Ages, in Germany, kissing a donkey was believed to relieve a toothache.

Fox: Also during the Middle Ages in Germany, it was said that if your teeth bothered you, you should run around a church three times without thinking of a fox.

Frog: Besides spitting in a frog's mouth for toothache relief, these web-footed creatures were applied to a person's cheek or to the head on the side of the ailing tooth.

Hog: Take a piece of the stomach of a newly butchered pig, wrap it in a rag, and apply it to the gums for thirty minutes.

Louse: Drill a hole in a dried bean and place a living louse in it. Close the hole with wax and suspend the bean from the neck. A live louse was also deposited into the cavity of an aching tooth in the hope of a cure.

Mole: The ancient Romans used to tear out a mole's tooth and carry it tied to the body to stop toothaches.

Mouse: To be cured of toothache, bite off the head of a living mouse and suspend it from the neck, but beware of making a knot in the thread or in the ribbon upon which it is suspended. To have good teeth, eat from bread that was gnawed by a mouse, especially at the very place that shows notches from the rodent's teeth.

Owl: If you pick your teeth with the nail of the middle toe of an owl, toothaches will never occur.

PLANTS AND ROOTS

Cloves: This spice was rubbed on sore gums. Oil of cloves is still used in dental materials today.

Garlic: The ancient Greeks considered a mixture of garlic, the resin from pine wood, and incense to be a good remedy for toothache, if kept in the mouth. The ancient Chinese had a favorite prescription of roasted garlic mixed with horseradish. This was made into a paste, using human milk. The paste was rolled into pills and inserted into the nostril on the opposite side of the aching tooth.

Henbane: This plant was used from earliest times as a fumigation for toothaches. Its seeds were mixed with sheep tallow to form small balls. The person would stand or kneel near a brazier (a pan holding burning coals) and hold a funnel with the large opening over the fire and the small end directed toward the tooth. The seed balls were dropped on the fire. The burning vapors that entered the tooth were supposed to drive out the worm.

Onion: In the Middle Ages a slice of onion was applied to the ear on the side of the aching tooth.

Parsley: A root of parsley was hung from the neck in the Middle Ages as a talisman against toothache.

17

A drawing from the late Middle Ages in Western Europe, showing a patient bending over a brazier containing burning henbane seeds. The purpose was to cure the toothache by driving out the toothworm.

Rye: Rye flour wrapped in a small linen bag and heated was tied to the cheek in case of toothache.

HUMAN ORGANS AND SECRETIONS

Bones: Go silently at midnight into a churchyard and bite the bone of a skeleton. It was recommended that the bone of the right thigh be rubbed on the aching tooth.

Fat: An aching tooth should be rubbed with human fat for relief.

Hand: Touching the aching tooth with the hand of a dead person was considered powerful magic, granting immediate relief.

Lips: A safeguard against toothache was to kiss the lips of an infant before it was baptized and kissed by anyone else.

Teeth: Touching the aching tooth with a dead man's tooth was a remedy tried during the Middle Ages and later.

Urine: The first urine of the morning was used as a medical mouthwash from ancient times through the eighteenth century.

INORGANIC

Arsenic: The ancient Chinese made arsenic into pills and placed them near the aching tooth or into the ear on the opposite side of the tooth.

Iron: Relieve a toothache by inhaling fumes produced by pouring oil on red-hot iron.

Lead: Place a used lead bullet, which had passed through a deer or some other game animal, under the person's tongue to get rid of a toothache.

Salt: The ancient Hebrews believed in applying a grain of salt to the aching tooth. In ancient Greece, salt was

19

considered helpful in the cure of ulcerated gums. In modern times we still use salt mixed with warm water to heal irritated gums.

Water: A warm foot bath was used in ancient times to relieve a toothache. A more recent bit of advice, also involving water, was definitely intended for humor: To get rid of tooth pain take a mouthful of cold water and sit on a hot stove until the water in your mouth begins to boil. You won't feel any pain in your tooth by that time.

THE TRANSFERENCE OF TOOTHACHE

Besides the toothache remedies listed above, there were other practices designed to transfer the demons causing a toothache from the sufferer to some other object. Trees were the most popular receivers of transferred toothaches.

In toothache transference, the demon was obtained by poking the gums with a nail or a splinter until it bled. Then the blood-stained nail or splinter was hammered into a tree. The demon would lose its powers because it was locked in the tree with no hope of escaping and returning to its victim. This method was used for other conditions of ill-health in addition to toothaches.

The use of a coffin nail or hobnail for transference was common among the ancient Romans and throughout the Middle Ages. In some countries the following phrase was recited while driving a bloody nail into a tree:

Nail, I complain to thee,
My tooth, it bothers me,
In me it leaves,
In thee it stays,
It won't have anything to do with me forevermore.

Sometimes the transference of toothache to a tree did not need to have a nail hammered into it. In Germany, a sufferer would kneel down in an orchard in front of a pear tree just before dawn and say:

Pear tree,
I complain to thee,
The red worm is pricking me.

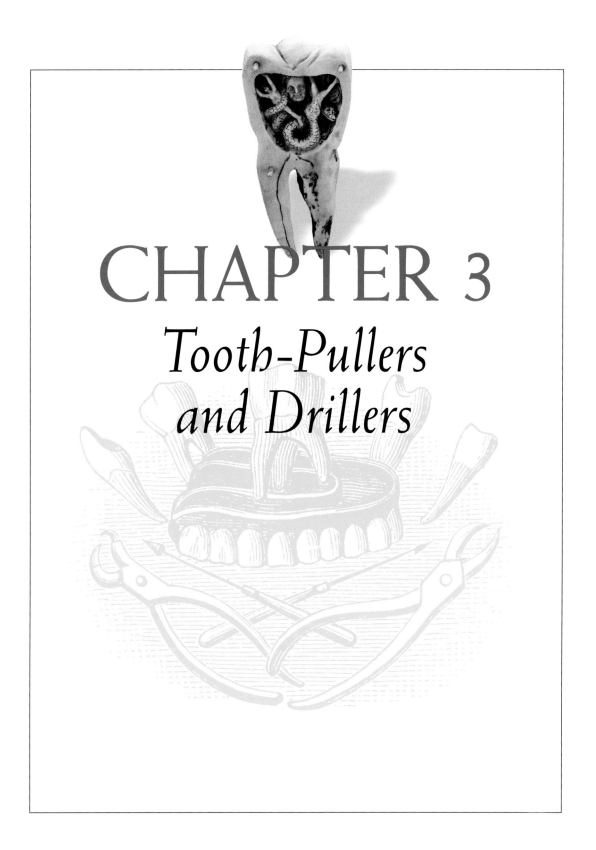

CHAPTER 3
Tooth-Pullers and Drillers

What happened when none of the magical cures or folk prescriptions stopped a toothache? The tooth was extracted (taken out). In many early civilizations, the sufferer took out his own tooth or had his neighbor do it.

One of the more primitive methods of extracting a tooth was to place a chisel-shaped piece of wood against a tooth and pound it with a mallet. This method was chancy because often only the crown portion of the tooth broke off, leaving the infected roots still inside the gum.

In ancient China, people called tooth-pullers removed teeth with their fingers, which they strengthened for the task by spending hours pulling nails out of planks.

Later on, pliers-like instruments made of iron, called forceps, were the most commonly used dental tool for extractions.

When an abscessed tooth was taken out, sometimes the fumes of burning hashish, opium, and certain hemlocks were given for the pain, but their use was not widespread and often nothing was done to numb the tooth. If more than one tooth needed to be extracted, the patient sometimes had to be chased down and held. Pulling teeth by inexperienced hands was also dangerous, many times resulting in broken jaws, the spread of infection, and even death.

During the reign of Hammurabi (about 1792–1750 B.C.), the sixth and best-known ruler of the First Dynasty of Babylonia, legitimate doctors began to treat medical and dental ills with surgery and medicines. Though these Babylonian physicians were rewarded generously, if successful, it was a risky profession. The following are two of four codes of laws that punished them if they injured their patients:

Law 200: If someone knocks out the tooth of an equal, his own tooth is knocked out.

Law 201: If someone knocks out the tooth of an inferior, he is fined a third of a mina of silver.

In Egypt the practice of medicine was established more than 4,000 years ago. The Egyptian civilization recorded medical information of the time on papyrus in hieratic writings. The Georg Ebers Papyrus (1550 B.C.) contains many references to dental ills, including gingivitis, erosion, pulpitis, and toothache. Though the Ebers Papyrus makes no mention of surgical procedures for these dental ills, the Edwin Smith Papyrus (1600 B.C.) does tell of operations for fractured and dislocated mandibles, compound fractures of the maxilla, facial bone fractures, and lacerated lips. Both of these papyri contain material originating from as far back as the earliest dynasty in Egypt, about 3100 B.C.

The first-known dentist was an Egyptian named Hesi-Re. His title was Chief of the Toothers and the Physicians. He lived about 3000 B.C. and specialized in dentistry. Wall carvings of forceps and knives show that Hesi-Re and others like him primarily extracted teeth. They also appeared to have been skilled in drilling holes through the cortical plates of the jawbones. Many skulls were found with these holes. One of the oldest skulls found, dating from the Old Kingdom (3100–2181 B.C.),

An Egyptian wood relief shows Hesi-Re, the first-known dentist, surrounded by some of the tools of his trade.

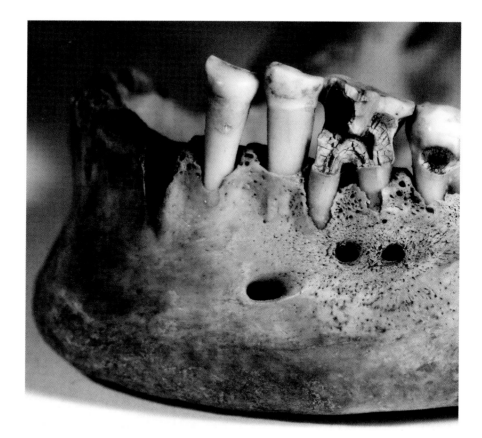

There is evidence of dentistry in this Egyptian jaw from about 3,000 years ago. Note the two holes drilled under the first molar, presumably to relieve pressure from around the root of a diseased tooth.

had two holes of the exact same size and depth, apparently drilled into the jaw to relieve the pressure caused by the buildup of pus from a tooth with severe caries.

In ancient Greece, a man named Hippocrates (about 460–377 B.C.) was considered the greatest physician of antiquity and is still referred to as the Father of Medicine. He claimed that disease was not the result of supernatural causes needing magical cures. It was, rather, a fault of nature, which could be corrected by physical and chemical agents. Besides writings related to the body, throughout Hippocrates's works are discussions of tooth formations and treatments. Dentistry and medicine were not separate professions in ancient times. Hippocrates explained the state of health and disease by naming four main fluids in the body, called the cardinal humors: blood, phlegm, black bile, and yellow bile. He also stated that four elements affected health as well: cold, heat, dryness, and moisture. All these humors and elements had to be in balance for a person to be healthy, according to Hippocrates. If anything, like too much phlegm, caused the humors and elements to be out of balance, then disease took place. It was from these teachings that the treatment of bloodletting became a common medical treatment to get the body in balance again.

Hippocrates conducted all his studies without examining a corpse or doing any kind of dissection. During ancient times the human body was considered private and sacred. No autopsy or study of the inner anatomy was permitted. Because of these restrictions, Hippocrates didn't look inside people's mouths and count their teeth before proposing the mistaken theory that men had more teeth than women.

Hippocrates also believed that tooth decay was caused by mucus and food attaching themselves to teeth with an inherited weakness. He recommended extractions of abscessed teeth only if they were loose; otherwise the operation was too dangerous for the patient. When it was necessary to pull a loose tooth, Hippocrates felt that the Greek forceps, called odontagra, were easy to use and could be handled by anyone.

In ancient Rome as in Greece, the Roman doctor made no distinction between diseases affecting the mouth and teeth and those of other parts of the body. What was unique about the Roman physicians was that women were allowed in the profession and were considered equal to their male colleagues.

The Roman encyclopedist Celsus (about 25 B.C.– A.D. 50), described in detail the surgical instruments used by the physicians of his day, including forceps and an instrument called a tenaculum for extracting the roots of teeth.

Besides doing extractions, early physicians sometimes filled decayed teeth. Roman doctors invented the technique of drilling into a decayed tooth and filling the cavity with a drug to ease the pain. One of these fillings was made of black veratrum, a plant with sedative qualities, mixed with honey.

Unlike our strong fillings today, like silver amalgam or light-cured composites, those of early civilizations were soft materials and did little to strengthen the teeth. But often they stopped the pain by insulating and keeping out air from the open cavity. The one exception was the more permanent filling called silver paste, which the ancient Chinese developed in the second century A.D. It was similar to the silver amalgams developed by dentists in the West more than 1,000 years later.

Here are a few examples of the strange and not so strange tooth filling materials used by doctors of ancient times and the Middle Ages: paprika, pepper, wax, the brain of a partridge, earwax, stone chips, turpentine resin, gum, metals, and ground bone.

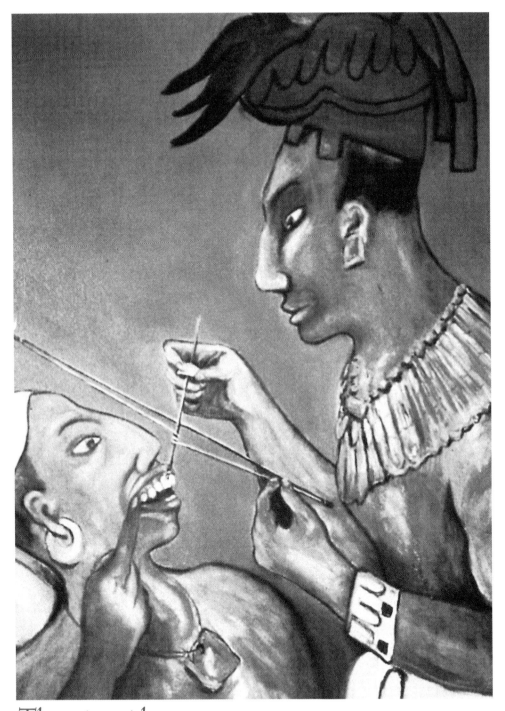

There is evidence that the bow drill was used as early as the first century A.D. by the Mayans, perhaps to prepare teeth for inlays.

What were early dental drills like?

The first drills were pieces of hard stones sharpened to a fine point and twisted into the tooth. Then came drills made of thin metal rods, turned by hand or rolled between the palms. Bow drills were one of mankind's first inventions and were used to make holes in many things before early dentists and surgeons found them useful. The bow drill looks like a small bow and arrow with a string tied across its opposite ends. Instead of an arrow, there is a drill made of a long, straight, thin metal rod. A handle, hollow like a tube, is attached to one end of the drill. To operate the bow drill one hand holds the handle as the other strokes the bow back and forth, like a violin, while the string winds, twists, and reverses, turning and pushing the drill into a tooth to make a fine hole.

All these early drills had limitations because they were awkward to use on back teeth. It was also hard to see in the mouth without modern dental lights and mouth mirrors.

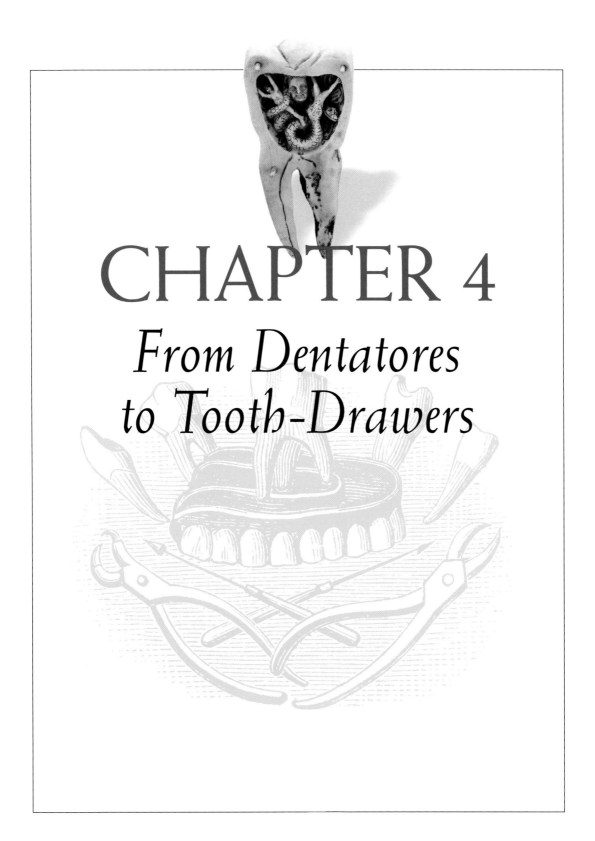

CHAPTER 4
From Dentatores to Tooth-Drawers

After the Roman Empire collapsed in A.D. 476, much of the medical and dental knowledge gained in ancient times was forgotten in Europe. Only the belief in the toothworm persisted as a scientific fact.

Most of the high-quality physicians in the Middle Ages were either Muslim or Jewish. The Arabs and the Jews were the only ones who preserved the scientific learnings of the ancients, and using this knowledge they were able to make many of their own advances in medical and dental techniques.

One of the greatest Arabian surgeons was Abul Kasim, (about 936–1013), who was called Albucasis in the West. He contributed much to dental science by concluding that calculus on the teeth was the major cause of periodontal disease and must be scaled off. He designed special instruments and methods to scale off the deposits. Albucasis also developed better and safer ways to extract a tooth by making fine tools, including elevators, forceps, and lancets for loosening the gums.

During the Middle Ages, from the fifth century to the fifteenth, surgeons who treated teeth were called dentatores. They specialized in removing decay from teeth, filled cavities with ground bone, repaired loose teeth with metal bindings, did extractions, and made partial dentures. But these surgeons were hard to come by, and only the wealthy could afford the cost of a real dentatore.

Most of the people living in the Middle Ages used one of the following groups of people for extractions: monks and priests, barbers and barber-surgeons, or tooth-drawers.

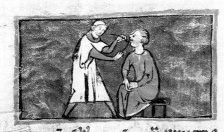

A panel from Albucasis's Surgery *showing that dental work was definitely one of his concentrations.*

MONKS AND PRIESTS

In Europe during the Dark Ages, the Catholic Church took control of thought and learning. The Church Fathers held to the belief than any illness or toothache was the result of punishment from God and not from natural causes. Because there was a need, monks and priests began to help the ill by performing surgery and doing tooth extractions. But the Church Fathers felt that the monks were spending too much time on medicine and not enough on clerical duties, so in the twelfth century they were forbidden to do any more surgery.

BARBERS AND BARBER-SURGEONS

Since monks were not allowed to practice medicine and dentistry anymore, this duty was assumed by the barbers who had assisted the monks in their surgical procedures.

Barbers became a versatile group in the Middle Ages and in later centuries. In addition to shaving beards and cutting hair, they lanced abscesses, did bloodletting, gave enemas, and extracted teeth.

Some of these barbers liked working on teeth and other ailments so much that they became barber-surgeons. To advertise their services of bloodletting, they displayed buckets of fresh blood in their windows. When the blood congealed, it was poured into the street, where it spoiled. In later centuries, instead of using real blood, red (symbolizing blood) and white poles were displayed in front of barber-surgeon shops to let people know that they did bloodletting.

This sixteenth-century engraving of a barber shop is somewhat satirical, in that it shows people not only getting their hair cut, but also having wounds treated, blood let, and teeth pulled—all in one easy stop!

There was a class distinction between the different medical professions. Many physicians looked down on surgeons. They considered surgery or body cutting akin to the work of a butcher, a manual job beneath their dignity. Trained surgeons, like Albucasis the Arab, looked down on barber-surgeons. And barber-surgeons, in turn, considered regular barbers beneath them.

35

TOOTH-DRAWERS

Tradesmen who specialized in pulling teeth were called tooth-drawers. They traveled from town to town and extracted teeth in outdoor booths and on stages at fairs or markets. The tooth-drawers distinguished themselves from other tradesmen by the way they dressed, wearing pointed caps and necklaces made of teeth they had pulled.

Going to a tooth-drawer for an extraction was not taken lightly. People had to be in terrible agony before letting a tooth-drawer touch them. Tooth-drawers had a reputation for being rough when extracting a tooth. Many of them were charlatans and quacks, who pretended to have great surgical and dental skills when they had little.

Dishonest tooth-drawers were in the habit of tricking the public in order to gain patients. When arriving in a new town they would gather a crowd around them to demonstrate how gentle they were. The tooth-drawer would call up a tooth-sufferer onto the stage. Within minutes after the tooth-drawer had put his hands inside the person's mouth, the sufferer was spitting out a bloody tooth. It looked so easy, but what the crowd didn't know was that the "sufferer" had been paid to pretend he had a toothache. The tooth-drawer had hidden a tooth in his hand, smeared with chicken blood, that had been quietly dropped into the actor's mouth. When a real sufferer went up on the stage, he found himself withering in pain and screaming at the tooth-drawer's rough methods—but the crowd was usually so loud that he couldn't be heard.

36

An etching from France in the late 1700s shows a tooth-drawer set up on a platform on Market Day. A display of false teeth helps draw a crowd. Notice that the poor patient is having his pocket picked while suffering at the hands of his performance-minded "dentist."

Even the honest tooth-drawers had limited skills and were capable of tearing large pieces of bone off with a tooth, breaking jaws, and causing facial deformities.

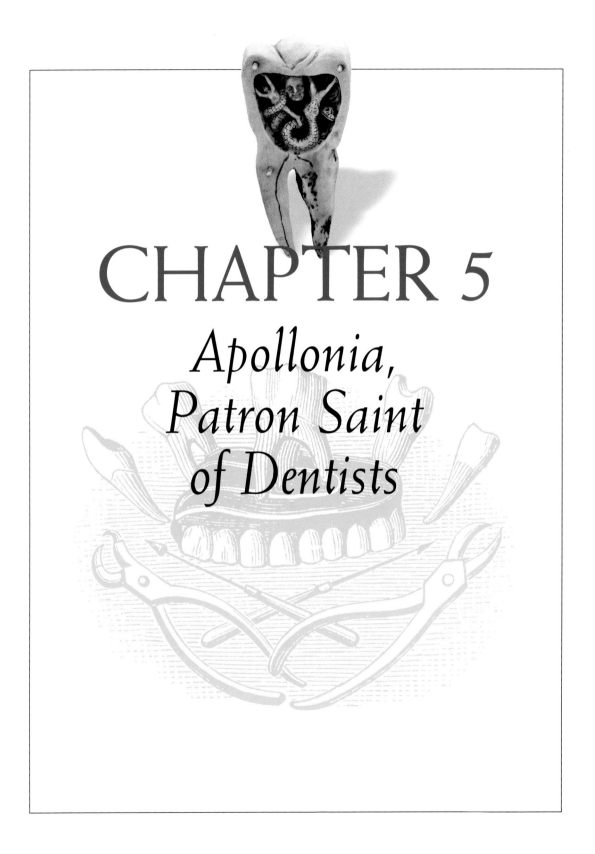

CHAPTER 5

Apollonia, Patron Saint of Dentists

In the Middle Ages it was common for people to die from dental infections. Since dentistry was still primitive and sanitary procedures were unknown, it was not only the tooth-drawers who could cause life-threatening infections by using dirty hands in a person's mouth or botching a surgical procedure.

During this time of dangerous dental treatments, people found themselves turning to St. Apollonia for spiritual help in their time of suffering. She was revered as the patron saint of toothaches. Apollonia was canonized in A.D. 249, and her feast day is still honored every year on February 9. But who was Apollonia, and how did she become a saint?

In the early days after Christ, the Church Fathers communicated by writing letters to each other. In one of these letters written by Dionysius, bishop of Alexandria, to Fabius, bishop of Antioch, the story of Apollonia was told:

Apollonia was born in Alexandria, Egypt, about two centuries after the death of Christ. She was the daughter of a prominent magistrate. Though neither of her parents was a Christian, Apollonia became a devout disciple of Christianity. She took to the streets of Alexandria and preached to crowds and gained many converts. During this time, the non-Christians in the Roman Empire were becoming fearful that the Church was gaining too much power, so Christians began to be persecuted and Apollonia was among them.

One day, mobs grabbed Apollonia and knocked out all her teeth, a common form of torture in Roman times.

39

This work (left) of French artist Ercole de'Roberti, dating from the late 1400s, depicts Apollonia, the patron saint of dentists, holding a set of forceps with a tooth in them.

A woodcut (above) from 1473 showing the martyrdom of Saint Apollonia. Her teeth are being knocked out with a mallet and chisel. The roots were pulled out with iron tongs. She was said to have prayed that in the future, all those who invoked her name for relief of tooth pain might be relieved from their suffering.

When they threatened to burn her alive if she didn't turn away from her faith and express belief in pagan things, she tore herself away from her captors and leaped into the flames. She died of her own free will, a martyr to her faith. While Apollonia was being burned, it was said that she called out to those who suffered from toothaches and promised them that if they appealed to her, she would relieve them of their pain.

After Apollonia was canonized as a saint, many churches and cathedrals had her likeness made into sculptures, stained-glass windows, and paintings. Even tooth-drawers had an insignia of St. Apollonia on their pointed hats. In all of this artwork, St. Apollonia is shown holding a tooth with forceps. Some of the forceps look like the ones dentists use today; others are much longer and resemble a blacksmith's tongs.

Even though Dionysius, in his letter, described Apollonia as elderly, she has always been depicted as a young and beautiful woman.

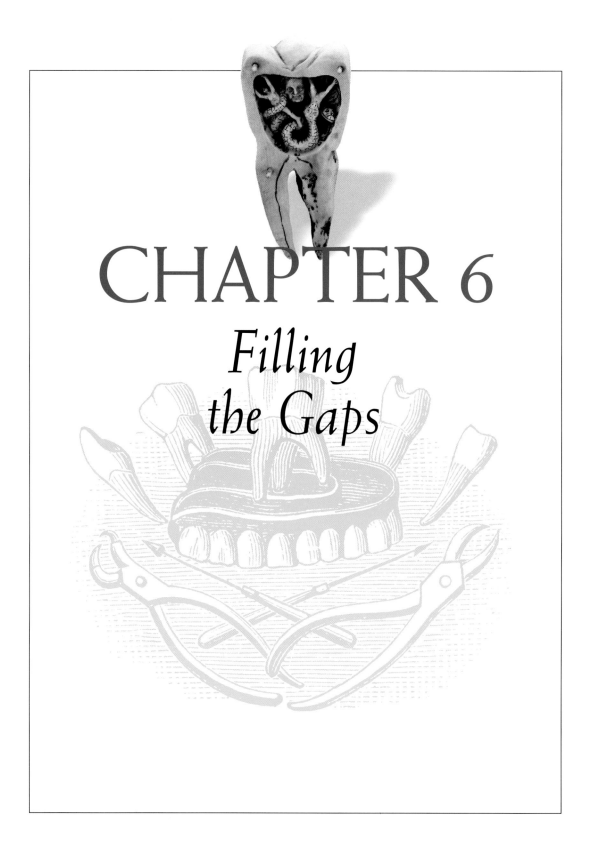

CHAPTER 6

Filling
the Gaps

For centuries many people, whether rich or poor, walked around with large gaps between their teeth because of tooth loss from decay and infections.

Even kings and queens had missing teeth. Queen Elizabeth I (1533–1603) of England filled the spaces in her mouth with cloth to make herself more attractive in public. In later centuries, women wore ivory balls, called plumpers, in the mouth to fill out their cheeks where teeth had been removed. They looked nice but found it hard to carry on a conversation.

People not only wanted to look good, but they needed to chew their food properly. Deaths from extractions were common, but so were those from digestive disorders. It is almost impossible to masticate food without good chewing teeth, like molars.

For thousands of years attempts were made—some successful, most not—at replacing missing teeth. Artificial teeth for filling empty spaces in the mouth have been found in jaws of ancient Egyptian remains. But no one is certain whether the wired teeth and fixed bridges were placed during the lives of these Egyptians or as part of the embalming process after their deaths.

The most advanced artificial dental appliances were made by the Etruscans. We know about their work from the jaw specimens found in their tombs. These skeletal remains survived the fires of cremation with gold bridges and crowns still in place.

The citizens of Etruria (about 800 B.C.) were a small nation in Italy before Rome became an empire. The Etruscans skillfully designed teeth out of ivory and bone and tied them to existing teeth with bands of soft, pure

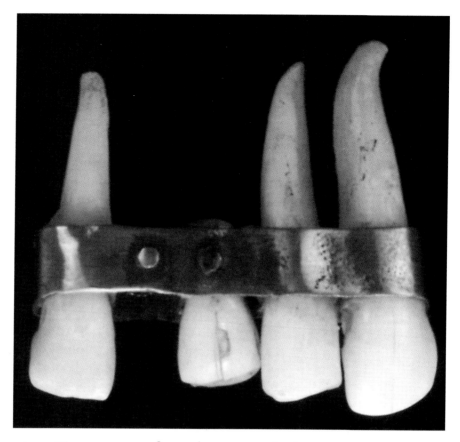

An Etruscan fixed partial denture on which the artificial tooth has been lost. Scientists surmise that the tooth of an ox was once riveted to the gold strap.

gold. They made other dental bridges using human teeth cut off at the gumline or teeth from calves and oxen. These teeth were fastened to the gold bands by rivets and fitted in the mouth next to the real teeth, making a fixed bridge.

The Etruscans eventually came wholly under the control of Rome in the early 200s B.C. The craft of making dental bridges and crowns was then carried on by the Romans. Most of this advanced dental work was done only for a chosen few. The majority of ancient people knew nothing about such craftsmanship.

After the fall of the Roman Empire, the excellent prosthetic work of the ancients was forgotten for centuries.

It wasn't until the 1500s that crude attempts were begun to replace extracted teeth. During this era, the first complete sets of dentures were made for people with no teeth at all. These early dentures were made of natural materials carved from cow teeth, elephant tusk, and walrus tusk. If human teeth were available, they were the material of choice.

How did early dentists get human teeth to use on these dentures? They were pulled from the dead or sold by poor people from their own mouths. Whenever a big battle took place, battlefield scavengers stripped corpses of their teeth. In the eighteenth century, "Waterloo teeth" were popular and in demand. These teeth were from soldiers killed during Napoleon's final defeat. The problem with using natural materials was their short life. Real teeth in dentures often rotted, turned brown, and made the wearer's breath smell like ten-day-old trash.

None of these early dentures fit well either. The major problems were finding the right materials, making accurate measurements of a person's mouth, and getting the teeth to stay in place. These first dentures were made for looks, not for chewing.

During the eighteenth century, transplantation (the placement of an extracted tooth into a socket other than its own) became popular, especially with dentists and quacks not skilled in making dentures or bridges. All

45

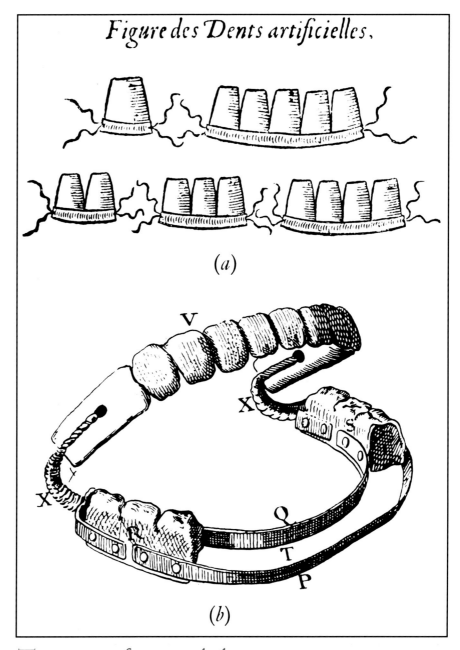

Figure des Dents artificielles.

(a)

(b)

Two sets of partial dentures, both from France.
*The top one dates from the sixteenth century, while the bottom one from
the eighteenth century. One can assume that they were both made from
ivory or bone—or perhaps teeth from cadavers.*

46

that was required in transplanting a tooth was a quick surgery with no follow-up later on to see how the patient was doing.

Getting the right teeth for transplanting was difficult because no two roots were exactly alike. Front teeth were easier to transplant because they had only one root and were more successful than molars with two to three roots. Higher prices were offered for teeth from living people because results were better. A poor person who wanted to sell a tooth for a transplant would come to the office and sit on one side of the dentist with a wealthy person on the other side. A tooth was extracted and transplanted in one appointment.

The need for good teeth for transplants led to the gangs of robbers, called toothnappers, who roamed the streets of France during the eighteenth century. These thieves watched people's mouths as they talked. Armed with forceps and sometimes a gun, they attacked and extracted, and later sold these stolen teeth to dishonest dentists and quacks.

As more and more of these transplanted teeth failed, people began to suspect them of transmitting diseases, such as syphillis. Despite this danger, the practice of transplanting human teeth continued well into the nineteenth century before it faded away, never to regain popularity.

In the eighteenth century, better dentures were developed. Fit and comfort improved in 1756 when Philip Pfaff (1715–1767), in Germany, introduced plaster of paris impressions of a patient's mouth. He did this by heating soft wax to take impressions of the jaw. Then

Pfaff mixed plaster of paris with water and poured it into the wax impressions where it hardened. After removing the wax, a rigid model of the patient's mouth was used to make the denture. There was no longer a need to work directly in the dark opening of a patient's mouth to make a denture.

This chapter would not be complete without discussing George Washington's dentures. First of all, none of them were wooden. Maybe this myth was started when some of his ivory dentures became stained from food and drink and resembled wood. Washington's favorite dentist, John Greenwood (1760–1819), advised him in a note written in 1798 that his stained dentures were "occasioned either by your soaking them in port-wine, or drinking it. Port, being sour, takes off all the polish. . . ."

Another source of the wooden-teeth myth may have come from the wooden pins that fastened the teeth to the denture base.

Washington wore dentures because he had lost one tooth after another to extraction. He suffered from toothaches all his adult life, and his famous quick temper may have been the result of this pain. By the time of his inauguration in 1790, Washington had only one tooth, his lower left bicuspid. A hole in his lower denture allowed this natural tooth to stick out. When it was time for Washington to sit for his presidential painting, the artist, Gilbert Stuart, thought that his dentures were too short, making his cheeks look sunken. He padded Washington's cheeks and lips with cotton to restore the natural lines to his face. But instead of looking better,

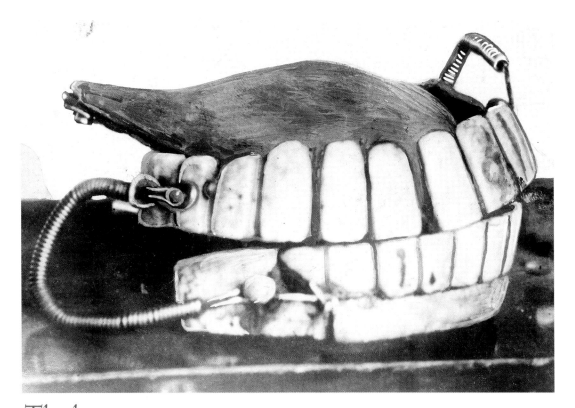

The last of George Washington's famous dentures—this one with a gold covered palate. Legend has the teeth made of wood, but actually the lower denture is carved from a single block of ivory, and the upper is ivory teeth riveted to the gold palate. The two were held together with a steel spring.

Washington has an overstuffed, grandmotherly appearance in his portrait.

Dr. Greenwood made at least four sets of dentures for Washington, and the father of our country was buried with one of these sets. The dentures were made of various materials like gold, hippopotamus ivory, elephant ivory, walrus ivory, cattle teeth, and human teeth. Upper and lower plates were held together with gold-alloy springs.

No matter what his dentures were made of, Washington found them uncomfortable and was constantly tinkering with them to improve their fit, as his letter to Dr. Greenwood indicates: "I sent you the old bars [denture bases], which you returned to me with the new set . . . you will find that I have been obliged to file them away so much above, to remedy the evil I have been complaining of as to render them useless perhaps to receive new teeth." December 12, 1798.

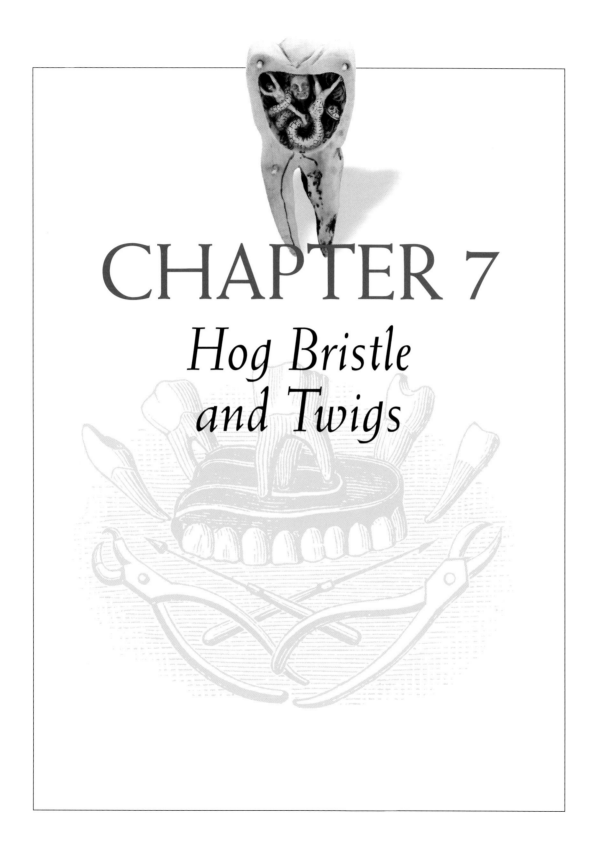

CHAPTER 7
Hog Bristle
and Twigs

As far back as prehistoric times, people had the urge to clean out the food crammed in between their teeth. What did they use before toothbrushes and floss were invented?

The following are what they cleaned their teeth with thousands of years ago and how those tools differ from what we use today:

TOOTHPICKS

The toothpick is probably one of the oldest dental cleaning tools. Prehistoric people may have used bone splinters as toothpicks and then thrown them away after one use.

In ancient times, more than 3,000 years ago, toothpicks were made from sharpened quill, wooden sticks, bronze, iron, silver, or gold. Babylonians in 2500 B.C. had hygiene sets consisting of a toothpick, tweezers, and ear scoop (to remove ear wax). The ancient Greeks used blades of straw and reeds to pick their teeth. A Roman woman of fashion always had a toothpick as part of her toilette.

Little is known of the use of toothpicks after the fall of the Roman Empire. When Rome fell and the Dark Ages took over, dental hygiene became less important. People in the Middle Ages were far too busy trying to save their lives and homes from battles, famines, and epidemics. Food was simply pulled out of the teeth with a knife or the fingernails.

It wasn't until the Renaissance period (1300–1600) that toothpicks became popular again with the rich (the

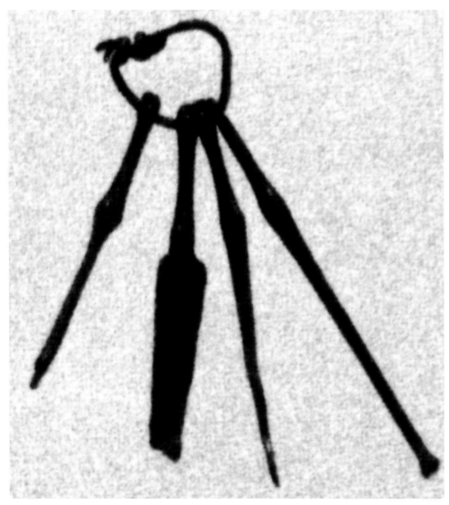

Archaeologists found this 4,000-year-old set of toilet articles, which includes a makeup applicator, an ear scoop, and a finely crafted toothpick, near ancient Nineveh.

poor couldn't afford them). During this time, pure gold toothpicks were carried in jeweled cases hung around the neck on a chain. It was considered good manners at court dinners to use a golden toothpick between courses to clean pieces of food from the teeth and spit them out loudly.

Toothpicks are still used today. Besides the popular wooden ones, we have plastic toothpick devices especially designed to fit between the teeth.

TOOTHPASTE AND TOOTH POWDER

Mixtures for cleaning teeth and freshening breath have been used since ancient times. Early Egyptian, Greek, and Roman writings describe many kinds of compounds for pastes and powders.

The first toothpaste or dentifrice was made in Egypt and consisted of wine vinegar and pumice.

The ancient Greeks used pumice, talcum, emery, granulated alabaster stone, coral powder, and iron rust for cleaning the teeth. Hippocrates mixed a tooth powder made of burnt hare's head and three mice.

In ancient Rome, pearly white teeth were so highly valued that slaves cleaned the teeth of their masters using a variety of powders and paste. These slaves were the first dental hygienists. They picked tartar off the teeth with special instruments or sharpened sticks. Then they rubbed on a tooth-cleaning powder with their fingers, a soft cloth, or a sponge and finished with a water rinse. Some of these powders included one or more of the following ingredients: bones, hooves and horns of animals, crabs, eggshells, and lizard livers. After burning these ingredients, honey or urine was sometimes added before the mixture was pounded into a powder. Many of the powders and pastes used in early times were so rough that they corroded or scratched the enamel, exposing the dentin layer underneath. Unlike enamel,

54

dentin is a living tissue and when exposed can cause tooth sensitivity and become decayed.

By the 1800s, modern toothpaste made its first appearance. Then, in 1956, fluoride was added to dentifrice to help prevent tooth decay. Today most toothpastes contain the following ingredients: abrasives (minerals), binders (natural gums), colors (natural and artificial), detergents, flavors (spearmint, etc.), fluoride, humectants (moisturizing agents such as glycerin), preservatives, and sweeteners (saccharin or sorbitol).

TOOTHBRUSHES

In 4000 B.C., the Hindus of India were the first people to use a toothbrush. It was made of a fresh twig with one end frayed into fibers.

Similar to the Hindu brush were the primitive chew sticks with mashed ends found in ancient Egyptian tombs.

In ancient China, a brush made of hog's bristle was used to clean teeth. This type of brush came to Europe during the seventeenth century and was soon widely used.

In 1938 nylon brushes with plastic handles were invented. The popular nylon bristles were of uniform height and easier on the teeth and gums than the hog bristles.

Nowadays, people have more choices than ever before in choosing a toothbrush. You can pick from many different styles and colors (even glow-in-the-dark ones) of soft nylon bristle brushes. There's also the more costly electric toothbrush that just about does the brushing for you.

Gazing into her mirror, an open box of tooth powder in front of her, a Japanese woman of about 1830 brushes her teeth with the end of a beaten twig.

FLOSS

In 1989 anthropologists digging at a site in Krapina, Yugoslavia, discovered evidence that prehistoric people may have flossed their teeth. Teeth found at this dig were grooved with tiny but regular, symmetrical channels. On seeing these evenly shaped marks, the anthropologists speculated that animal sinews or tendons may have been used as prehistoric dental floss.

Today dental floss is basically a string that comes unwaxed or waxed, or as a tape. It may be flavored with mint, cherry, grape, or cinnamon. Using a length of floss to wrap around each tooth is like shining a shoe and is considered the best way to clean between the teeth.

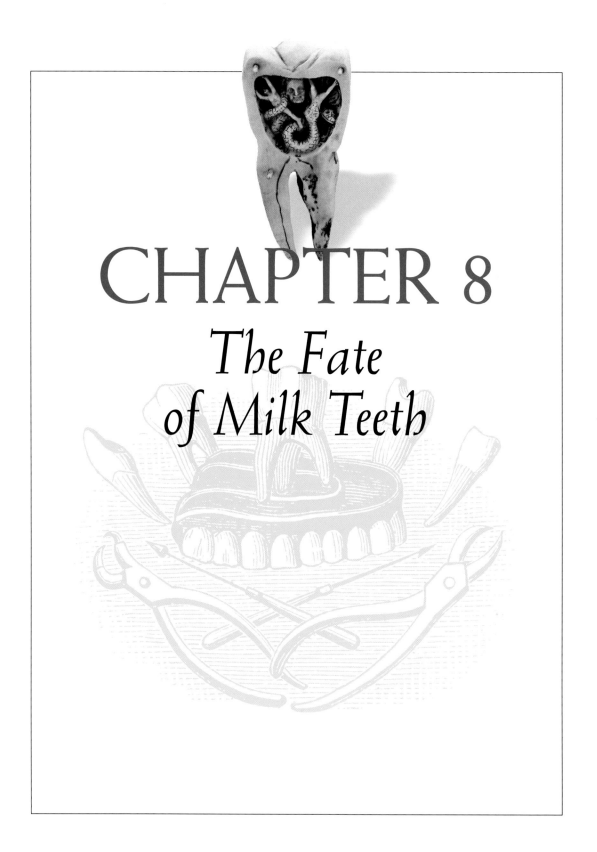

CHAPTER 8

The Fate of Milk Teeth

Here are some commonly known tooth facts that the ancients didn't know about: The first set of teeth you get as a child are called either baby, primary, or deciduous teeth. The average age for cutting a first tooth is six months. When babies reach two years of age, they have a full set of twenty primary teeth. By the time children are about six years old, they lose their first deciduous teeth and begin to cut permanent teeth. Usually between the ages of seventeen and twenty-four, most people have a full set of 32 permanent teeth.

Though most early people didn't know how many teeth they had, they were aware of the eruption of their children's first teeth. They called them milk teeth because it was thought, at the time, that teeth grew from the milk flowing onto the baby's gums from the breast of a nursing mother.

On rare occasions, if a baby was born with erupted teeth, it might be killed as a demon.

When it was time to shed these milk teeth, early cultures had certain rituals to be followed for their proper disposal. These customs were strictly carried out because it was believed that the health, strength, and whiteness of the permanent teeth depended on them. The following are some of those rituals:

The Mouse Connection: If a milk tooth falls out, children should throw it backward over a shoulder into a mouse hole, over a roof, behind furniture, onto a straw roof, or anywhere that a mouse would be sure to find it. The wish is that the mouse would take the tooth and give the child a strong one, like the mouse's own sturdy teeth.

Around the late nineteenth century in France, the mouse's role changed. No longer did it take the milk tooth with the hope of replacing it with a stronger one. Instead, the tooth mouse traded the shed tooth for a small present or a coin.

Other Animals: Though the mouse was a highly popular rodent, other animals were also expected to bring a child a new and stronger tooth. Any sharp-toothed animal would do, such as a rat, squirrel, beaver, or dog.

Sun: In earlier times, Arabian boys took their lost milk teeth between their fingers and thumbs and threw them toward the sun, saying: "Give me a better one for it."

Gulping Them Down: In some cultures, mothers swallowed their children's milk teeth to save them from having toothaches in their permanent ones.

Trees: In other old cultures, the father who wishes to save his child from toothaches for life takes the first lost tooth out to a forest early in the morning. With no one seeing his actions, the father inserts the milk tooth in the hole of a willow tree, closes the hole carefully with a wooden plug, prays, and leaves, believing that his child's permanent teeth will never ache.

Tooth Fairy: In the United States, parts of Canada, Spain, and Great Britain, belief in a tooth fairy became popular at the beginning of the twentieth century. The ritual involves placing the shed baby tooth under a pillow. The child wakes up to find money in its place.

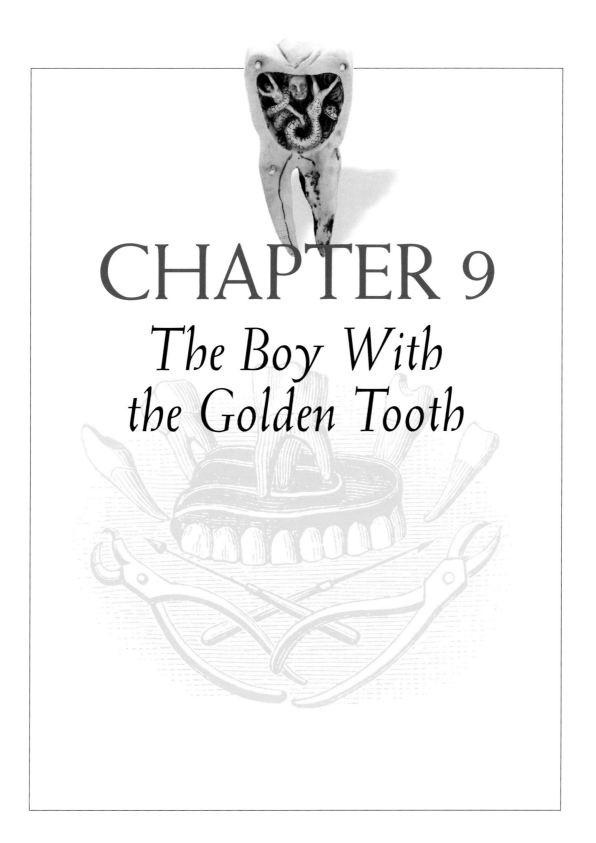

CHAPTER 9
The Boy With the Golden Tooth

In 1593 in a small town near Silesia, Germany, an astonishing discovery was made. A seven-year-old boy named Christoph Muller was found with an erupted gold tooth in his mouth. The thick molar was behind the rest of his upper left teeth.

People came from all over the country to view the tooth. It was examined by experts and found to be a highly refined grade of gold. Among the people who came to see the tooth was Professor Jacob Horst from the medical faculty at Germany's University of Helmstedt. When Dr. Horst decided to write a book about the gold tooth, he created even more widespread attention for Christoph by saying that the gold tooth was a sign from heaven. By his astrological calculations, on Christoph's birthday, December 22, 1585, the sun was in conjunction with Saturn in the sign of the Ram. This caused a great heavenly burst of heat, which turned the tooth into gold instead of hard bone. Dr. Horst gave many university lectures explaining his theories on the appearance of Christoph's gold tooth.

Many believed Dr. Horst without question, while others differed with his interpretations. And some thought he was a fool or a faker, and the tooth a complete trick.

Christoph's father, a poor carpenter, allowed examination of his son's tooth for a payment. His circumstances improved with the income. Though people were permitted to look, whenever knowledgeable men wanted to study the gold tooth, Christoph would go into sudden fits of madness, making the viewing of his tooth impossible.

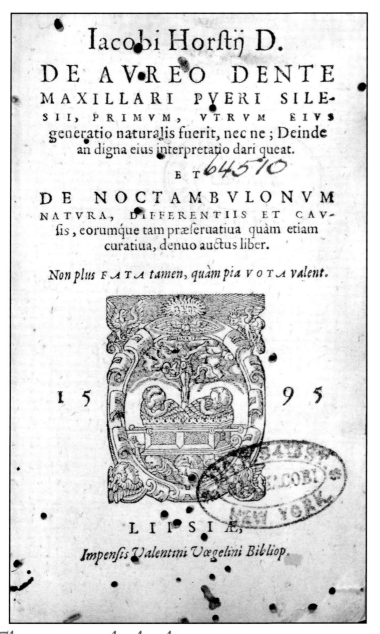

Iacobi Horstij D.

DE AVREO DENTE
MAXILLARI PVERI SILE-
SII, PRIMVM, VTRVM EIVS
generatio naturalis fuerit, nec ne ; Deinde
an digna eius interpretatio dari queat.

ET *64510*

DE NOCTAMBVLONVM
NATVRA, DIFFERENTIIS ET CAV-
fis, eorumque tam præferuatiua quàm etiam
curatiua, denuo auctus liber.

Non plus FATA *tamen, quàm pia* VOTA *valent.*

1 5   9 5

LIPSIÆ,
Impenfis Valentini Vœgelini Bibliop.

The very scholarly looking title page of Dr. Horst's book on Christoph's golden tooth. An approximate translation of the subtitle is: "The golden tooth of the maxillary of the child of Silesia {the first question being to know} if its creation was natural {the second} if correct interpretation can be done."

One day, a doubting nobleman held a dagger to Christoph's face, forcing him to open his mouth. After looking carefully, he saw that the natural tooth was showing through the worn cusp area of the gold. The gold tooth proved to be a hoax. It was really a well-fitting gold shell that covered the real tooth underneath. The boy was sent off to prison without anyone knowing who made the golden crown and placed it in his mouth. Many were angry with the disclosure, choosing to still believe in the gold tooth.

Eighty years later, in 1673, another boy, this time a three-year-old in Poland, was found to have a gold tooth. But after careful study of the boy's tooth, it appeared more yellow than gold. It turned out to be a massive buildup of tartar, and the bishop of the town ordered the deposit removed.

As time went on, people began to question happenings in their lives, like these "naturally occurring gold teeth," by using reason and science. The era of superstition and ignorance was starting to fade, and the age of Enlightenment was beginning.

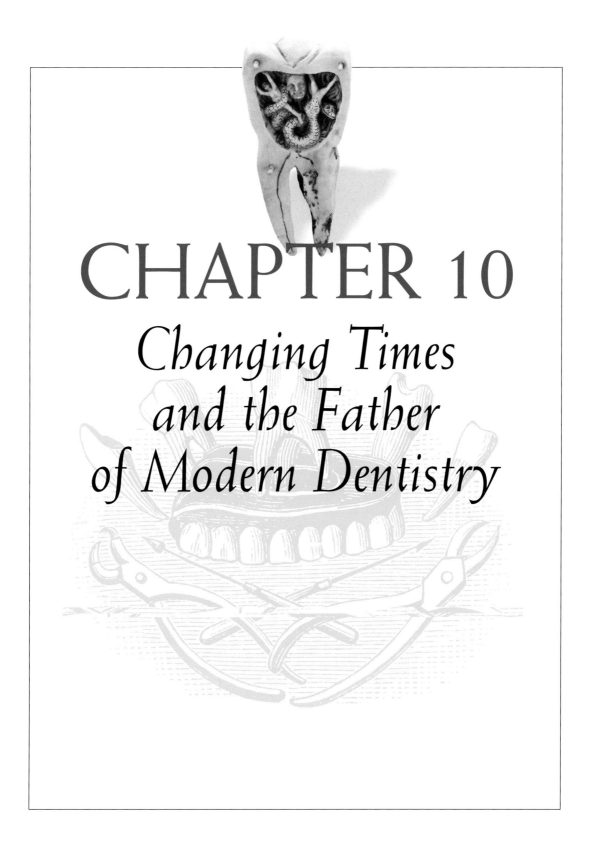

CHAPTER 10

Changing Times and the Father of Modern Dentistry

In 1683 the Dutch naturalist Anton van Leeuwenhoek was shocked when he turned his newly invented microscope on scrapings from the teeth. He saw "animalcules" (bacteria) in such great numbers living on the teeth that he was at a loss for words. He finally asserted that the vast amount of microscopic life in a human mouth far exceeded the number of men living in his country.

When the eighteenth century rolled in, the scientific data from Leeuwenhoek and the work of a dentist named Pierre Fauchard helped give birth to true dentistry.

In the early 1700s, Paris was one of the greatest centers of science and culture. Wealthy people came from all over the world to enjoy the city and its entertainments. Having an attractive appearance with nice teeth became important. It was during this time that the founder of modern scientific dentistry, Pierre Fauchard (1678–1761), wrote his far-reaching book on dentistry. This remarkable Frenchman had trained as a military surgeon and dentist, before settling in Paris. He organized dentistry for the first time into an independent profession, separate from the medical field and, more important, from the trade of the tooth-drawers. In 1723 he completed a book, *The Surgeon-Dentist*, or *Treatise of the Teeth*, although it was not published until 1728. It was the first complete book on dentistry ever written. A second and even better edition consisting of 843 pages divided into two volumes, was published in 1746. This was an unusual book for its time because other practitioners never gave away or shared any of their knowledge, keeping it a well-guarded secret. Here are a few of the many dental issues discussed in this book, some of which are still current today:

Pierre Fauchard's publication of The Surgeon-Dentist, *a book detailing complex dental instruments and methods, earned him the title of founder of modern dentistry.*

67

Toothworm Theory: Fauchard rejected the long-held toothworm theory as the cause of decay. He claimed he had never seen a toothworm, either with the naked eye or a microscope. Trying not to offend past writers on the toothworm, he mentioned that if it did exist, it was not the cause of tooth decay. Insects' eggs from overripe food may have entered the cavity and hatched, producing worms (maggots). Fauchard believed that the real cause of tooth decay was "humoral imbalance." He stressed the importance of keeping the teeth clean because dental health affected the whole body.

Education: Fauchard emphasized the need for specialized dental education. He had no respect for tooth-drawers, calling them a "theater of impostors" who tricked people. He also blamed bad dentistry on procedures practiced by unqualified people from unrelated professions offering oral-health services.

Periodontal Disease: Fauchard was far advanced, for the times, in his understanding of periodontal disease. He was a firm believer in scaling teeth and debridement of root surfaces.

Extractions: In his book, Fauchard describes five kinds of instruments he used for extractions, which were available to all dentists: the gum lancet, the punch, the pinchers, the lever, and the pelican. He found the pelican the most useful because it took out a tooth more promptly than the others. But he warned that if someone didn't know how to handle it, the pelican could be the most dangerous of all instruments in drawing (extracting) teeth.

Orthodontics: Fauchard proposed methods that laid the groundwork for modern orthodontics. He realized the need to align teeth in the jaw because crowded teeth were hard to clean and caused decay, infection, periodontal disease, and tooth loss.

Bridges and Dentures: Fauchard was highly skillful in prosthetic work. He made drawings for his book to show how he used silk, linen, and metal threads to fasten artificial teeth and bridges to neighboring teeth.

Fauchard recommended using human teeth or teeth carved from walrus or elephant tusks for dentures. He also developed ways to keep upper and lower dentures in place by joining them together with springs. Though these dentures had a lot of drawbacks, like springing out of the mouth while the wearer was talking, his pioneer work in coloring and enameling denture bases to simulate natural gum tissue inspired later dentists to make more lifelike dentures.

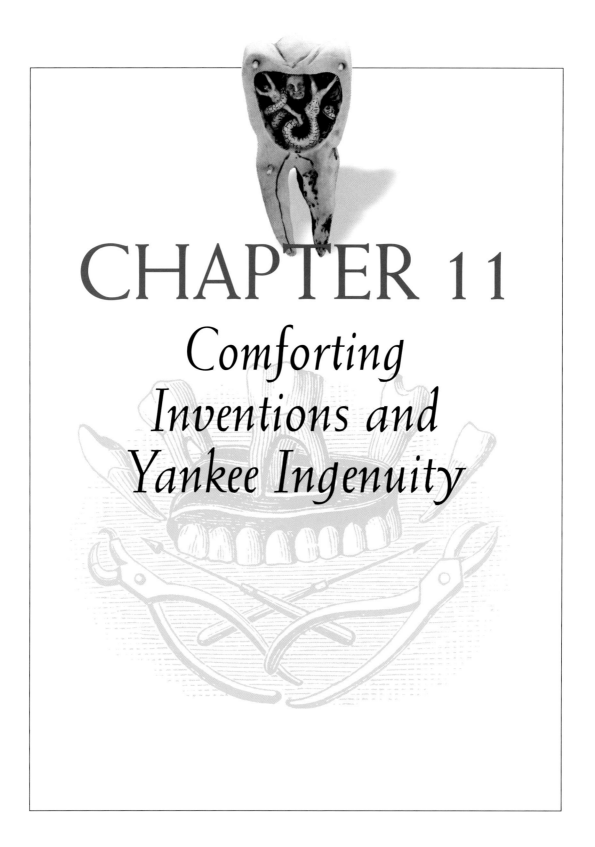

CHAPTER 11
Comforting Inventions and Yankee Ingenuity

If you needed a dentist in colonial America you would have gone to the local blacksmith, wigmaker, barber, or anyone else who did dentistry on the side. From the early 1600s through the 1700s, most colonists in America had no access to professionally trained dentists. As a result, many colonists suffered from tooth ailments. When home remedies didn't work, these early Americans had little choice but to go to one of these part-time dentists. One of the most famous of these was Paul Revere (1735–1818). Besides being a master silversmith, engraver, and patriot, he practiced dentistry by doing fillings, cleanings, and constructing bridges and dentures.

By the end of the 1700s, more and more medically trained dentists had relocated to America. After arriving in the New World, they traveled from town to town, letting people know of their coming by announcing themselves on posters and handbills and in newspapers. They would advertise with phrases like "Painless Dentistry by Dr. ———."

One of the first native-born, full-time dentists in America was Josiah Foster Flagg (1763–1816). Some reports say that he was trained either by Paul Revere or by a Frenchman named James Gardette. Josiah Flagg practiced a full range of dental skills from prosthetics to orthodontics. His most notable contribution to dentistry was the invention of the dental chair. He took an ordinary Windsor chair and added a headrest and an extended armrest for holding instruments.

The great influence that Americans had on dentistry came with the founding of the Baltimore College of

American-born dentist Josiah Flagg was the inventor of the first dental chair. It doesn't appear to be much of an invention—just a headrest and instrument tray attached to a regular chair—but it was a considerable advance in comfort and convenience from earlier set-ups.

Dental Surgery in 1840. It was the first dental college in the world. Formal dental training in modern techniques at the school made the United States the world leader in dentistry.

Besides the white dentists practicing in America at the time of the opening of the Baltimore College of Dental Surgery, about 120 African-Americans were practicing dentistry. These African-American dentists had learned their trade by working as apprentices under white dentists. In the 1800s not many white dentists would work on African-American patients, so there were opportunities for black dentists.

72

In 1869, Robert Tanner Freeman made history by being the first African-American to get a proper dental education. Denied entry into independent dental schools, he was in the first class of six students to graduate from the Harvard University School of Dental Medicine.

In 1881 the Howard University College of Dentistry in Washington, D.C., was founded to educate African-American dentists. In 1886 another college, Mebarry Medical College, in Nashville, Tennessee, also began educating African-Americans to be dentists. These two colleges were responsible for training African-American dentists in the United States until desegregation in 1954. From then on, no student could be refused entrance into any dental college because of his or her race.

What about women? Were there any women dentists in early America? Way into the nineteenth century, few women practiced dentistry unless a male family member taught them to assist with their patients. None of the newly formed dental schools would admit women as students. But then in 1866, after much determination and a refusal to give up, Lucy Beaman Hobbs graduated from the Ohio College of Dental Surgery in Cincinnati, the first woman in the world to obtain a dental degree.

Ida Gray was the first African-American woman to graduate from the University of Michigan School of Dentistry and receive a dental degree in 1890.

The nineteenth century brought many breakthroughs in dentistry, and many were American inventions. One American, Charles Goodyear (1800–1860), discovered vulcanized rubber in 1839, which aided in the making of dentures. Goodyear, working in his birthplace of New Haven, Connecticut, received a patent for the vulcanized rubber in 1844. This cheap, easy-to-work material could be molded to fit the mouth and made a good base to hold false teeth.

One of the greatest contributions to the medical and dental fields was by an American dentist who, in 1844, discovered the practical use of anesthetics. Before that time, people had to endure surgical operations and dental treatments without anything to numb the pain. Horace Wells (1815-1848), a dentist in Hartford, Connecticut, discovered a way to use nitrous-oxide gas on his patients when doing extractions. He experimented on himself first by having another dentist come to his office with an inflatable bladder (rubber bag) to administer the gas. Wells inhaled the gas and became unconscious. When he awoke, he found that one of his teeth had been extracted without any discomfort. His discovery allowed him to perform needed extractions on patients who had stayed away because of fear. At this time, however, dentists had no way of telling how much gas they were giving a patient because they had nothing to regulate it. Dangerous overdoses were common.

Because of the fear of giving patients too much gas, Horace Wells lost his followers when he demonstrated an extraction on a man who had not been given enough of the gas to deaden the pain. Wells was called a fraud, and the gas went into disfavor for decades. Unable to bear the criticism and lack of appreciation for his discovery, Wells committed suicide at the age of thirty-three. In 1864, after his death, Horace Wells was finally given recognition by the American Dental Association

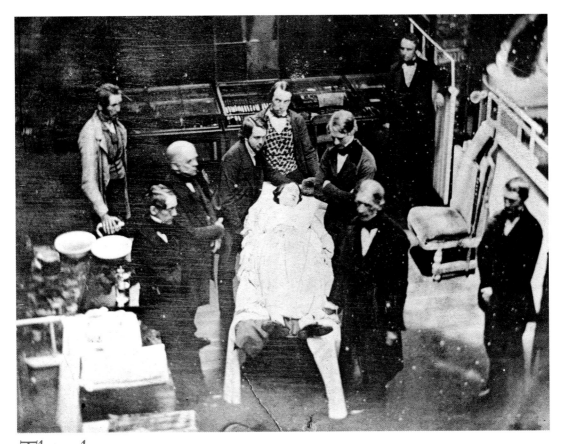

This daguerreotype was made at the second operation performed under ether anesthesia, on October 17, 1846. At the head of the table, in the checkered vest, is dentist William T. G. Morton administering the anesthesia.

and the American Medical Association for his work in the development of anesthetics.

Another American dentist to discover an anesthetic for practical use was William Morton (1819–1868) of Boston. He did the first successful demonstration of ether anesthesia. He first experimented with animals before trying it on a human. He administered the drug with a glass globe into which a sponge saturated with ether had been placed. The patient became unconscious after inhaling the drug, and Morton was then able to extract a tooth without hurting the person. But Morton, like Wells, never received immediate credit for discovering a use for ether anesthesia, and ended up with a ruined dental practice. He died a pauper in 1868.

At present, ether is no longer used in most medical and dental settings, but nitrous oxide is still administered to patients who request it. If the gas is used, it is given not to make patients unconscious, as in earlier times, but to get them into a relaxed state while awake during their dental procedures. Nitrous oxide is contained in a tank and delivered from a gas system combined with oxygen into a nosepiece. Gauges and valves regulate the dosage safely. After the dentist completes his or her work, the gas is shut off and the patient is given only oxygen to breathe, clearing out all traces of the gas.

The use of local anesthetics, given by injection, began in 1858. These drugs, developed from cocaine, numbed the tongue, took away feeling and taste, and made the fully awake patient comfortable and pain-free. The first of these drugs was Novocain, but by 1948, Xylocaine became the most commonly used local anesthetic in dental offices.

Another big leap in the advancement of dentistry came in the nineteenth century by yet another American dentist, Willoughby D. Miller. Miller was educated at the University of Pennsylvania. He later became the first foreign professor at the University of Berlin, Germany, where, in 1890, he discovered that acids were created on the teeth after food mixed with bacteria and its by-products in the mouth. The acids decalcified the enamel on the teeth, bacteria entered the hole, and

Inventions by American Dentists Outside the Field of Dentistry

Dentist Thomas Bramwell Welch (1825–1903) of Vineland, New Jersey, created an unfermented grape juice in 1869 that he called "Dr. Welch's Unfermented Wine."

In 1869, William F. Semple (1834–1922), a dentist in Ohio, was the first inventor to patent chewing gum. Semple hoped that people would be able to clean their teeth with it.

Dentist William James Morrison (1860–1926) of Nashville, Tennessee, invented the cotton candy machine, called the Fairy Floss Machine, in the nineteenth century. The machine that he designed still works today just as it did then.

decay resulted. Miller's initial theory was carried further by later dentists until it was understood that this accumulation of tooth-destroying acid, which is called plaque, must be removed daily or it will multiply, causing cavities and gum problems. Dentists began teaching preventive measures by advising the use of antiplaque toothpastes and mouthwashes, and stressing flossing and brushing, plus regular professional scaling.

Besides the American dental inventions and theories, one other major discovery that contributed to changing dental and medical treatments forever was made by a German physicist named Wilhelm Roentgen (1845–1923). He developed the use of X rays by discovering that rays from electric currents could penetrate solid objects. When he exposed photographic films to these invisible beams, a shadow picture of the object appeared. The first radiographs, or X-ray photos, of teeth were taken in 1896 by physicist Walter Konig in Frankfurt, Germany. Soon many experiments were

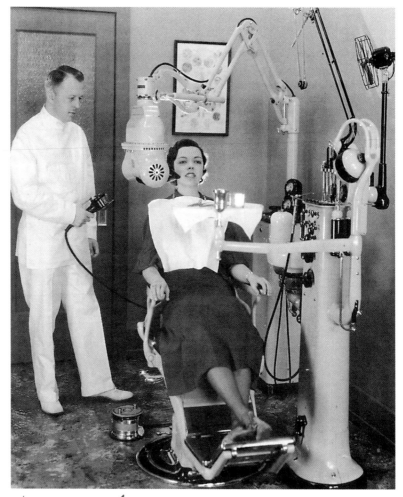

A 1940 advertisement for the well-equipped dental office, showing a female patient having X rays. Unfortunately, the profession was not yet aware of the dangers of radiation, so the technician is standing nearby and the patient is not covered with a lead apron as is required today.

done, with no one knowing that long, daily exposure to the X-ray beams could cause malignancies (cancer). Early Xray machines were crude and slow, taking as long as twenty minutes or more for exposures.

One American dentist in the 1890s, Dr. C. Edmund Kells of New Orleans, Louisiana, held film plates positioned in the mouths of hundreds of patients while taking X rays of their teeth, ignorant of the damage the beams were doing to his hand. First he lost his three fingers to cancer, then his whole hand until his suffering led to suicide. He was one of many "X-ray martyrs" of the time.

Nowadays, patients in dental offices are covered with lead aprons to prevent penetration of the beams to their bodies while their teeth are X rayed with an approved X-ray machine. Only a short exposure time, a fraction of a second, is required to take an X ray.

Modern dentistry has changed over the past hundred years into a profession that treats patients gently and without a lot of discomfort. High-speed drills do procedures quickly, and local anesthetics do a good job of making the patient feel numb. Root-canal therapy, in many cases, can be performed to save abscessed teeth from being extracted. Fluorides in drinking water, rinses, pills, fillings, and toothpastes have made a major impact in preventing decay. Dentures are now made of plastic or porcelain and constructed to fit perfectly in the mouth, without need of springs. Crowns, bridges, veneers, and implants are amazingly natural-looking. Skilled orthodontists successfully straighten crowded teeth and align jaws.

The next time you visit your dentist for a checkup, look around and see how far dentistry has come from the days of toothworms and spider juice!

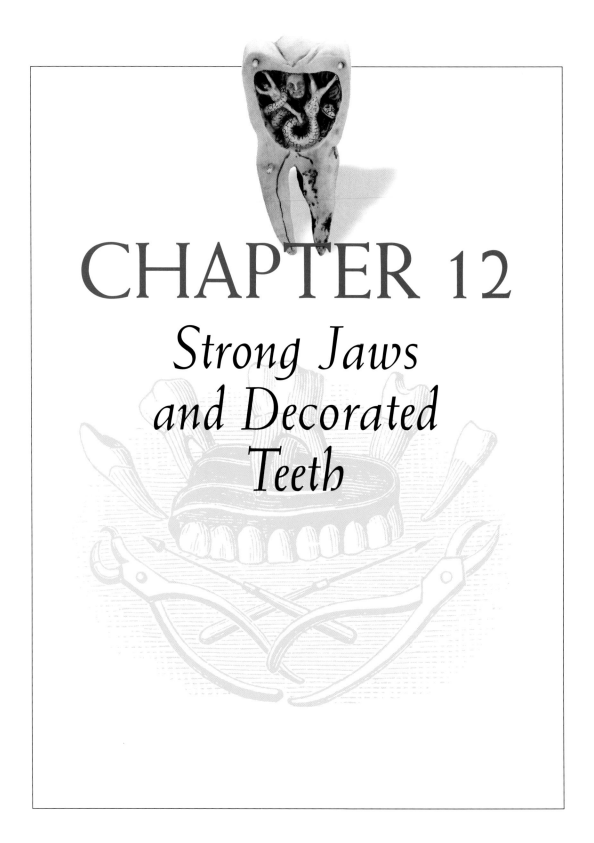

CHAPTER 12
Strong Jaws and Decorated Teeth

In the previous chapters you have read about tooth disease, remedies, modern inventions, and how important teeth are for chewing, talking, and smiling. But did you know that some people today make a living with their teeth? Or that certain cultures follow ancient practices of beautifying their teeth by changing their color or shape?

Let's look first at the people whose job depends on them having strong and healthy teeth:

Iron-Jaw Acts: The muscles in the jaw can put out hundreds of pounds of force. With this in mind, a circus act called the "iron jaw" routine was created many years ago. An aerialist (a person who performs feats in the air) holds the end of a rope with her teeth while suspended high in the air. The iron-jaw mouthpiece attached to the rope is essential to the success of the act. The first mouthpiece was constructed about 150 years ago. It was just several layers of leather sewn together to fit the contours of the inside of the performer's mouth. The semicircular leather pad was then attached to a swivel that hung from a suspended web. The performer bit as hard as possible into the leather while being lifted in the air. The aerialist then proceeded to spin around, bringing many cheers from the awe-struck audience below.

When modern dental plates made of plastic and nylon were introduced in the 1930s, better and safer mouthpieces were constructed for the women performers, who did most of the iron-jaw acts. Impressions were taken of the woman's mouth, and stone casts were made of the exact shape of her lower and upper teeth. From

Aerial artists thrilled circus crowds with their ability to spin about while hanging from their teeth.

82

these casts, a full upper and lower set of plates, without the teeth added, was made. The plates had holes drilled in them so that they could be sewn onto a long leather strap folded in half to fit the performer's full bite. Because the mouthpiece was custom-fit, only the show-girl for whom it was made could use it.

One of the greatest dangers to the iron-jaw act was gagging. The mouthpiece filled the whole mouth, and, until the performer got used to it, choking was common. Problems also occurred when aerialists hung vertically, causing their tongues to fall in the backs of their throats. They had to practice overcoming this natural tendency. Another great hazard was when the mouthpiece chipped or broke during a performance.

Some of the most famous iron-jaw performers were Barbette (1902-1973), a female impersonator born Vander Clyde Broadway in Round Rock, Texas, and Antoinette Concello (1912-1984), born in Burlington, Vermont. Another circus aerialist, Penny Wilson from Florida, became an iron-jaw performer at the age of twelve in the early 1950s. She used a mouthpiece custom-made of a hard rubber shoe heel, a strip of leather, and a metal hook. She would hang in the air dressed as a human butterfly and thrill the crowds. Wilson's mouthpiece is on display at the Dr. Samuel D. Harris National Museum of Dentistry in Baltimore, Maryland. Marks from her teeth and traces of her lipstick are still on it.

Other related acts were performed by men and women raising and lowering other performers and horses with their teeth. Some even held chairs and tables between their teeth and lifted them over their heads.

Bill Pickett Used His Teeth: A famous African-American rodeo star named Bill Pickett (1870–1932), who invented the art of bulldogging or steer wrestling, did a startling trick with his teeth. Pickett brought spectators to their feet when he rode his horse alongside a steer, jumped off the horse, grabbed the steer around the horns, and wrestled it to the ground. As the animal struggled, Pickett bit down on its lower lip and jerked the animal flat. After that he let go of the steer and received a resounding ovation from the crowd.

Teeth Decoration: Since prehistoric times, certain societies and ethnic groups have decorated their teeth with jewels, sharpened them to a point, colored them, or even knocked them out. They used their teeth as a fashion statement, like some people use tattoos on their skin. Tooth alteration for the most part is done as a rite of passage, mourning a loved one, or maybe for group identity and to conform to their idea of beauty. A few of the following tooth-decorating practices still exist in some parts of the world:

🦷 In ancient Mayan societies (A.D. 300–900), inlays of jade and turquoise were placed in the front teeth for ritual or religious purposes and not to restore the teeth.

🦷 In ancient Japan, women dyed their teeth black. They used tannin powder and a ferrous acetate solution. It was a sign of fashion and marital status and was practiced into the early twentieth century. Though the women didn't know it, the coloring they used helped protect their teeth from bacteria.

🦷 Placement of gold crowns over front teeth and open-faced gold crowns with cutout designs called

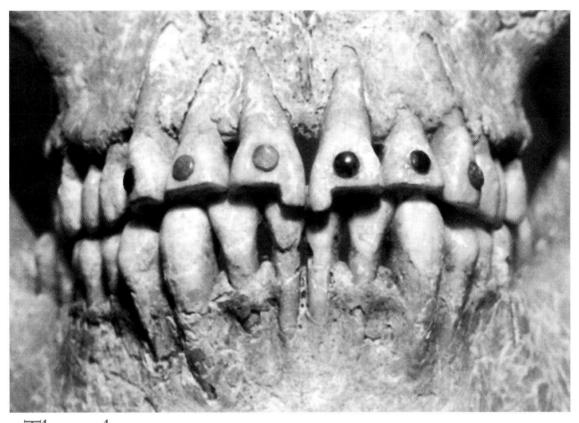

The teeth of this ninth century A.D. Mayan skull have inlays of jade and turquoise.

windows have been popular for years, especially in some cultures in America.

■ Knocking out teeth, not because of infection or as a form of torture, but as part of a rite of passage or a sign of mourning was once carried out by some Australian tribes.

■ Certain South American Indians of the Amazon Valley file their front teeth to points to imitate the feared piranha fish that live in their rivers. They also think that sharpened teeth are a mark of beauty.

Modern Western cultures have their own view of beautiful teeth. White teeth are most admired in these societies. Dentists make available to anyone who desires whiter teeth bleaching agents to lighten them. Impressions are taken to make custom-fit plastic trays that fit over the teeth. These trays are filled with a gel made of carbamide peroxide, which is capable of making teeth seven to eight shades lighter. The color change lasts from one to three years.

If you look in the mirror, you may find that plain old teeth are pretty fine, too!

SOURCE NOTES

When doing the research for this project, I came upon several fascinating books on the history of dentistry. If I had to pick favorites, I would say that three of them stand out in my mind as the richest sources of information. The first, *Dentistry: An Illustrated History*, by Malvin E. Ring, gave me the information for Chapter 1 on the lore of the toothworm and how ancient cultures dealt with their belief in its existence. Besides the folklore of the toothworm, this book gave me an excellent overview of all aspects of historic dentistry. I found myself referring to it often to confirm information that I had discovered in other texts. The second, a wonderful old volume titled *Folklore of the Teeth*, by Leo Kanner, provided many of the gross toothache remedies listed in Chapter 2. It also was a good source in Chapter 8 on the fate of milk teeth, and in Chapter 9, on the boy with the golden tooth. The third, *Teeth, Teeth, Teeth: A Treatise on Teeth and Related Parts*, by Sydney Garfield, gave me quirky facts that went into Chapters 2, 3, 4, 6, and 7. Dr. Garfield's illustrations were also invaluable in my understanding the evolution of the dental drill discussed in Chapter 3.

Besides using book sources, written material sent to me from The Dr. Samuel D. Harris National Museum of Dentistry and visual displays I was able to see firsthand at this museum in Baltimore, Maryland, provided me with the information about Washington's dentures in Chapter 6, inventions by American dentists in Chapter 11, and much of the information in Chapter 12 about circus acts and decorated teeth.

GLOSSARY

Abscessed Tooth: Infection caused by bacteria getting into the pulp of a tooth.

Anesthesia: The loss of sensation or feeling in a body part. In *general anesthesia*, the central nervous system is altered temporarily so that sensation is lost throughout the entire body, making the patient unconscious. In *local anesthesia*, only certain, selected nerve pathways of a body part lose sensation while the patient remains conscious.

Bicuspid: A tooth with two cusps (rounded areas on the chewing surface).

Bloodletting: An ancient remedy to treat disease. It required removing "bad" blood from a vein by making an incision or placing leeches on the body.

Bridge: A restoration that replaces missing teeth. In a *fixed bridge*, the restoration is cemented permanently to abutment teeth that support a span of one or more false teeth. In a *removable bridge*, the restoration is hooked around natural teeth and can be taken out of the mouth to be cleaned.

Calculus: Also known as *tartar*. It is made of calcium deposits, broken-down blood and mouth tissue cells, food debris, bacteria, and fungi and their toxins. This yellow-to-brown, stonelike substance develops and attaches itself to teeth at the gumline when plaque is left in place and not removed by a brush and floss.

Caries: The scientific word for tooth decay.

Cementum: A thin, hard bonelike substance that covers the root of a tooth. Unlike enamel, cementum is alive because it is connected to the blood vessels in the jawbone.

Charlatan: A quack or faker; one who pretends to have much knowledge and skill but really has none or very little.

Crown: The part of the tooth, covered by enamel, that is above the gum. A crown can also be a hollow, artificial cap that fits over a tooth to replace its natural crown.

Cuneiform: Written words composed of wedge-shaped characters.

Debridement: The removal of contaminated substances from the teeth, such as plaque, stain, calculus, and food debris.

Decalcified: Loss of calcium salts from bones or teeth.

Dentifrice: A compound made of paste or powder used with a toothbrush to clean the teeth.

Dentin: A yellowish bonelike tissue that forms the bulk of a tooth and is the body's second-hardest substance. Dentin surrounds the tooth pulp and is covered by enamel on the crown and by cementum on the roots. Dentin is alive and can repair itself because the bloodstream nourishes it.

Dissection: Cutting open a dead body to study its anatomy.

Elevator: A strong steel extraction instrument. A dentist inserts its sharp tip between a tooth's root and the fibers attaching it to the bone. The tooth is dislodged when the elevator is wiggled and rotated.

Enamel: A shiny hard tissue that ranges in color from light yellow to grayish white. Enamel covers all of the exposed teeth from the crown to the neck at the gum line. The hardest substance produced by the body, it is made of calcium, phosphorus, and other minerals.

Endodontist: A dentist who specializes in treating the pulp (nerve) of the tooth.

Erosion: A localized, progressive decalcification of enamel and dentin, especially on the front surface of teeth. These shallow, scooped out areas on a tooth are caused by a chemical action, like sucking on too many lemons or drinking vast amounts of acidic liquids such as carbonated sodas.

Fluoride: A chemical element occurring naturally in some drinking water. Fluoride is added to public water supplies, where needed, to prevent tooth decay. Fluoride compounds react with tooth enamel to make it more resistant to bacterial acid.

Gingivitis: An inflammation of the gums and the start of periodontal disease.

Hieratic: A cursive form of ancient Egyptian writing, simpler than hieroglyphics.

Hieroglyphics: Ancient Egyptian picture writing used by the priesthood in sacred carvings.

Impaction: Failure of a permanent tooth to erupt all the way through the jawbone and gum.

Implant: An artificial device that replaces the root of a missing tooth and then is used to anchor a crown, a bridge, or a denture.

Light-cured composite: A tooth-colored filling material made of a soft resin that can be placed into a tooth's cavity. The composite hardens when a bright light is shined on it.

Mandible: The lower jaw.

Masticate: To chew.

Maxilla: The upper jaw.

Occlusal: Pertaining to the biting surface of a tooth.

Orthodontics: The dental specialty of correcting the misalignment of teeth and dental arches to achieve a correct bite and maintain the health of the teeth.

Papyrus: Plants that grow in the waters of the Nile. In ancient Egypt the stems were cut into strips, wet, crushed together, and then dried to make long, rolled paper scrolls.

Georg Ebers Papyrus: A German Egyptologist, Georg Moritz Ebers (1837–1898), found a hieratic medical papyrus about 66 feet (20 meters) long that had been written in ancient Egypt around 1550 B.C. This famous papyrus bears his name after he and his group translated and edited the work in 1874.

Edwin Smith Papyrus: At the same time of the discovery of the Georg Ebers Papyrus, a group of men led by Edwin Smith found another papyrus medical record of ancient Egypt, dating from 1600 B.C.

Pelican: An extraction instrument that was used for centuries. It consisted of a fixed part covered with leather and a movable arm with a hooked end shaped like the long-necked bird called a pelican. The hooked end takes the tooth out while the fixed end pushes against adjacent teeth and acts like a brace.

Periodontal Disease: Disease of the gums and the supporting tissues of the teeth.

Plaque: The slimy combination of microorganisms, food debris, and mucus that sticks to the teeth. Considered to be a major cause of gum disease and tooth decay.

Plaster of Paris: A white powdery, finely ground gypsum, mixed with water to make a paste that is poured into casts or molds.

Prosthesis: An artificial device to replace missing parts of the body. In dentistry, a prosthesis replaces teeth, or any part of the oral structure lost to disease, birth defects, or accidents.

Prosthodontics: The dental specialty of replacing teeth with bridges and dentures.

Pulp: Soft, living tissue in the center of a tooth made of nerves, blood vessels, and connective tissue. It forms dentin and maintains the life of the tooth.

Pulpitis: Inflammation of the pulp leading to sensitivity to hot and cold and to pressure. It is the main cause of a toothache.

Pumice: A substance of volcanic origin, used in powdered form mixed with water as a polishing material.

Root Canal Therapy: A dental procedure that removes an infected pulp from the root canal (the space in the root that holds pulp tissue), cleans out the canal, and shapes and sterilizes it before filling the empty canal with a special material called gutta-percha.

Scaling: The careful and complete removal of plaque and calculus by the use of sharpened instruments.

Silver Amalgam: An alloy (mixture of two or more metals) of silver, mercury, copper, tin, and zinc used in dentistry for filling cavities in teeth.

Talmud: The written authoritative body of Jewish tradition, involving civil and religious laws.

BIBLIOGRAPHY

Anthony, Catherine Parker, and Thibodeau, Gary A. *Structure and Function of the Body.* St. Louis: C.V. Mosby Company, 1980.

Armento, Beverly J., Nash, Gary B., Salter, Christopher L., and Wixson, Karen K. *A Message of Ancient Days.* Boston: Houghton Mifflin Company, 1991.

Consumer Reports. *A Guide to Good Dental Care.* September 1992.
————. *Which Toothpaste Is Right for You?* August 1998.

Culhane, John. *The American Circus.* New York: Henry Holt and Company, 1990.

Davis, Peter. *The Social Context of Dentistry.* London: Croom Helm, 1980.

DeSantis, Kenny. *A Dentist's Tools.* New York: Dodd, Mead & Company, 1988.

El Mahdy, Christine. *Mummies, Myth and Magic.* New York: Thames and Hudson, 1989.

Enamel, *California Dental Health Magazine*, Spring, 1996, Vol. 1 No. 1: Receding Gums.

Garfield, Sidney. *Teeth, Teeth, Teeth: A Treatise on Teeth and Related Parts.* New York: Simon and Schuster, 1969.

Glenner, Richard A., Davis, Audrey B., and Burns, Stanley B. *The American Dentist: A Pictorial History with a Presentation of Early Dental Photography in America.* Missoula, MT: Pictorial Histories Publishing Co., 1990.

Kanner, Leo. *Folklore of the Teeth.* New York: The Macmillan Company, 1934.

Kenyon, Sherrilyn. *The Writer's Guide to Everyday Life in the Middle Ages*. New York: Writer's Digest Books (imprint of F&W Publications, Inc.), 1995.

Ogden, Tom. *Two Hundred Years of the American Circus*. New York: Facts on File, Inc., 1993.

Olmert, Michael. *Milton's Teeth and Ovid's Umbrella: Curiouser and Curiouser Adventures in History*. New York: Touchstone Books, 1996.

Pediatric Dentistry, Volume 11, Number 2, June 1989.

Ring, Malvin E. *Dentistry: An Illustrated History*. New York: Abradale Press, Harry N. Abrams, Inc., 1985.

Scherer, Warren. *Oral Care Products for the 1990s*. The California Dental Institute for Continuing Education, Herndon, VA, Vol. 47, 1993.

Schissel, Martin J., and Dodes, John E. *The Whole Tooth*. New York: St. Martin's Press, 1997.

Siegel, Dorothy. "Dental Health," *The Encyclopedia of Health*. New York and Philadelphia: Chelsea House Publishers, 1994.

Silverstein, Alvin, and Silverstein, Virginia B. *So You're Getting Braces: A Guide to Orthodontics*. New York and Philadelphia: J.B. Lippincott Company, 1978.

Stay, Flora Parsa. *The Complete Book of Dental Remedies*. Garden City, New York: Avery Publishing Group, 1996.

Travers, Bridget, and Muhr, Jeffrey. *World of Invention*. Detroit: Gale Research, 1994.

Wynbrandt, James. *The Excruciating History of Dentistry*. New York: St. Martin's Press, 1998.

INDEX

Page numbers in *italics* refer to illustrations.